Gertrude B. Elion
and Pharmacology

By Ellen Labrecque

21st Century
Junior Library

Published in the United States of America by
Cherry Lake Publishing
Ann Arbor, Michigan
www.cherrylakepublishing.com

Content Adviser: Amelia Wenk Gotwals, Ph.D., Associate Professor of Science Education, Michigan State University
Reading Adviser: Marla Conn MS, Ed., Literacy specialist, Read-Ability, Inc.

Photo Credits: © Dragon Images/Shutterstock Images, cover; © Darren Baker/Shutterstock Images, 4; © Bettmann/Contributor/ Getty Images, 6; © Everett Historical/Shutterstock Images, 8, 10; © David Litman/Shutterstock Images, 12; © Will And Deni McIntyre/Contributor/Getty Images, 14; © National Science Foundation/Wikimedia (EricSerge), 16; © Rigucci/Shutterstock Images, 18; © Monkey Business Images/Shutterstock Images, 20

Library of Congress Cataloging-in-Publication Data
Names: Labrecque, Ellen.
Title: Gertrude B. Elion and pharmacology / by Ellen Labrecque.
Description: Ann Arbor : Cherry Lake Publishing, 2017. | Series: 21st century junior library | Series: Women innovators | Audience: K to grade 3. | Includes bibliographical references and index.
Identifiers: LCCN 2016029706| ISBN 9781634721820 (hardcover) | ISBN 9781634722483 (pdf) | ISBN 9781634723145 (pbk.) | ISBN 9781634723800 (ebook)
Subjects: LCSH: Elion, Gertrude B.—Juvenile literature. | Pharmacologists—United States—Biography—Juvenile literature. | Women biochemists—United States—Biography—Juvenile literature. | Women medical scientists—United States— Biography—Juvenile literature. | Women Nobel Prize winners—United States—Biography. | Nobel Prize winners— United States—Biography.
Classification: LCC RM62.E43 L33 2017 | DDC 615.1092 [B]—dc23
LC record available at https://lccn.loc.gov/2016029706

Cherry Lake Publishing would like to acknowledge the work of The Partnership for 21st Century Skills.
Please visit *www.p21.org* for more information.

Printed in the United States of America
Corporate Graphics

CONTENTS

Scientists play a very important role in treating and curing diseases.

A Woman

Have you taken medicine when you were sick? Did it make you feel better? Scientists create these medicines, or drugs, to help people get well.

Gertrude B. Elion was one of these scientists. She helped make drugs that fight many diseases, including **cancer**!

Gertrude grew up with a thirst for knowledge.

Gertrude Belle Elion was born on January 23, 1918, in New York City. Gertrude's mom and dad were **immigrants**. Her dad was a dentist from Lithuania. Her mom was from Russia. When Gertrude was 15 years old, her grandfather died from cancer. She knew then that she wanted to fight this disease.

When Gertrude was growing up, most women didn't study science.
Laboratory work was usually reserved for men.

Gertrude entered Hunter College in New York City. She studied **chemistry** and graduated in 1937. After college, she wanted to work in a **laboratory**. She wanted to research new drugs to cure cancer. But she had trouble finding a job. Most scientists were men at this time.

Think!

Think about making a new medicine to beat a disease. What disease would it treat? How would the medicine work?

Teaching was a common profession for women at the time.

Elion worked at many different jobs. She even taught high school science. She soon went back to school and earned a master's degree in chemistry from New York University. Finally, she got a job working in a laboratory for a scientist named George Hitchings.

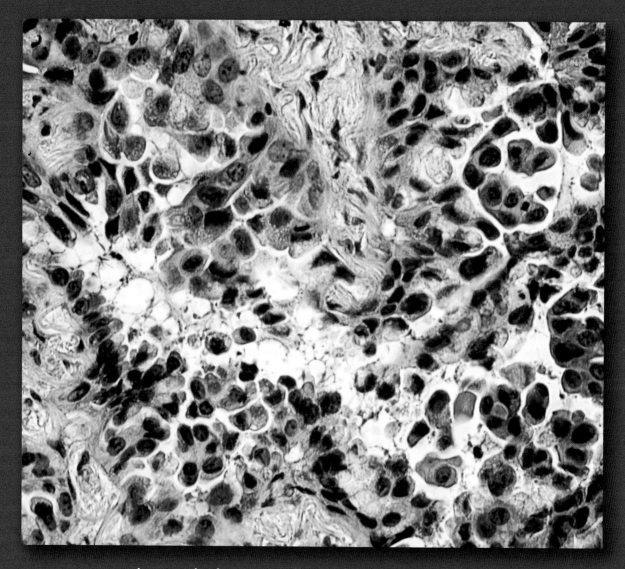

Elion studied cancer cells to learn how to kill them.

An Idea

Elion **invented** many new drugs. Her research was different than that done by other scientists at the time. Her medicines killed the diseases. But they did not harm the healthy **cells** in a person. This was different from other medicines. Some of them kill healthy cells while fighting the disease.

Elion and Hitchings worked together for much of their careers.

Elion made medicines that help cure some types of cancer. She also made drugs that help cure sick people of **infections**. In 1988, Elion and her research partners, George Hitchings and Sir James Black, won the Nobel Prize for their work. The Nobel Prize is the highest award a scientist can win. It is a wonderful honor.

Ask Questions!

Ask your teacher or librarian to tell you about another Nobel Prize winner. What did this person accomplish in his or her life?

A Legacy

In 1991, the president of the United States, George H. W. Bush, awarded Elion a National Medal of Science. Bush said that her work "transformed the world." That same year, she became the first female to be inducted into the National Inventors Hall of Fame. Gertrude B. Elion died in 1999. She was 81.

Every year, thousands of people participate in events like this one to fund cancer research.

Today, scientists work every day to come up with new medicines to cure diseases. Elion's drugs fight some cancers. But they don't beat all kinds. There is still much more work to be done.

Create!

Scientific research can be expensive. Can you create an event to help raise money? Is it a bake sale? Or maybe a talent show? Have your friends and family help out. See how much money you can raise.

Scientists invent medicines so that doctors can help people.

Scientists are like doctors behind the scenes. Without them working hard, doctors wouldn't have the medicines they need to do their job. Elion's **legacy** is that she devoted her life to helping other people get better. She worked in a field that is filled with men. And she was a shining star among them!

GLOSSARY

cancer (KAN-ser) a serious disease in which some cells in the body grow faster than normal cells and destroy healthy organs and tissues

cells (SELZ) the smallest units of living matter

chemistry (KEM-uh-stree) the scientific study of substances, what they are composed of, and how they react with each other

immigrants (IM-ih-gruhnts) people who move from one country to another and settle there

infections (in-FEK-shuhnz) disease-producing germs that make people sick

invented (in-VENT-id) created something new from imagination

laboratory (LAB-ruh-tor-ee) a room or building that has special equipment for people to use to do scientific experiments

legacy (LEG-uh-see) something handed down from one generation to another

FIND OUT MORE

BOOKS

Calkhoven, Laurie. *Women Who Changed the World*. New York: Scholastic, 2016.

Dee, Catherine. *The Girls' Book of Wisdom: Empowering, Inspirational Quotes from Over 400 Fabulous Females*. Boston: Little Brown, 1999.

MacBain, Jennifer. *Gertrude Elion: Nobel Prize Winner in Physiology and Medicine*. New York: Rosen Publishing, 2003.

WEB SITES

Live Science
www.livescience.com
A great site to check out the latest news in science.

Nobel Prize site
www.nobelprize.org
Find out more about Gertrude Elion and other Nobel Prize winners.

INDEX

ABOUT THE AUTHOR

Ellen Labrecque is a freelance writer living in Yardley, Pennsylvania. Previously, she was a senior editor at Sports Illustrated Kids. Ellen loves to travel and then learn about new places and people that she can write about in her books.